DATE DUE

MAR 3 0 2005		
AUG 0 6 2009		
DEC 1 5 2009		
NOV 2 3 2013		
AUG 2 0 2014		
MAY 0 8 2017		

Demco, Inc. 38-293

101 FACTS ABOUT

IGUANAS

Please visit our web site at: www.garethstevens.com
For a free color catalog describing Gareth Stevens Publishing's list of high-quality
books and multimedia programs, call 1-800-542-2595 (USA) or 1-800-387-3178
(Canada). Gareth Stevens Publishing's Fax: (414) 332-3567.

Library of Congress Cataloging-in-Publication Data

Williams, Sarah, 1976-
    101 facts about iguanas / Sarah Williams. — North American ed.
      p. cm. — (101 facts about pets)
    Includes bibliographical references and index.
    ISBN 0-8368-2888-7 (lib. bdg.)
    1. Iguanas as pets—Miscellanea—Juvenile literature. 2. Iguanas—Behavior—
Miscellanea—Juvenile literature. [1. Iguanas—Miscellanea. 2. Iguanas as pets—
Miscellanea.] I. Title: One hundred one facts about iguanas. II. Title. III. Series.
SF459.I38W56   2001
639.3'9542—dc21   2001031054

This North American edition first published in 2001 by
Gareth Stevens Publishing
A World Almanac Education Group Company
330 West Olive Street, Suite 100
Milwaukee, WI 53212 USA

Ringpress Series Editor: Claire Horton-Bussey
Ringpress Designer: Sara Howell
Gareth Stevens Editor: Heidi Sjostrom

Printed in Hong Kong through Printworks Int. Ltd.

2 3 4 5 6 7 8 9 05 04 03 02

101 Facts About

IGUANAS

Sarah Williams

Gareth Stevens Publishing
A WORLD ALMANAC EDUCATION GROUP COMPANY

2 Like all reptiles, a lizard is an **ectothermic**, or cold-blooded, creature. It cannot make its own body heat. It needs heat sources outside its body to make it warm enough to move.

1 All iguanas are lizards. They are part of a family known as reptiles, which also includes crocodiles, snakes, turtles, and tortoises. Lizards have been around for over 260 million years.

3 There are 700 **species**, or kinds, of iguanas, but the species most people keep as pets are common Green iguanas. Their scientific name is "Iguana iguana."

4 The name "iguana" comes from "iwana," which was the word that Caribbean Indians used to describe all lizards. Spanish explorers translated "iwana" into "iguana" – and the name stuck.

5 All species of iguanas are now **endangered**. Because people eat their meat and their eggs, destroy their **habitats**, and capture them for pets, laws have been made to protect them.

6 Baby iguanas hatch from eggs that a female iguana lays and buries in an underground burrow. A group of iguana eggs is called a clutch. Each clutch can contain 30 to 50 eggs.

7 Newborn iguanas are about 7 inches (18 centimeters) long.

8 Some Green iguanas get very big. Adults can be up to 7 feet (2 meters) long and can weigh up to 18 pounds (8 kilograms).

9 Most iguanas have the same basic body structure and living habits. Some live in trees, while others live on the ground.

10 To help them balance in trees, most iguanas have long tails. An iguana's tail can be two or three times longer than the rest of its body.

11 An iguana's toes and claws help it hold on to tree branches. Iguanas' toes are called **digits**. Each of their front feet have five digits, just like people's feet, but their back feet have only four digits.

14 Central America has some Green iguanas with gray heads. In South America, some have red heads. Some have very pale green heads that look white.

12 Iguanas have two eyes on their faces and a third eye, called a parietal eye, on top of their heads. This third eye does not see the way normal eyes see, but it does recognize changes in light and dark.

15 Iguanas are usually bright green when they hatch, but that color fades as they get older.

13 Green iguanas are not always green! Some are brown, and, in at least one area of South America, some are blue.

17 The Chuckwalla iguana is a lot like the Green iguana, but it is much fatter. Chuckwallas live in the deserts of the southwestern United States.

16 The Green iguana (above) can be found in South America, Central America, northern Mexico, the Antilles Islands, and, more recently, in the United States, especially in Florida.

18 The Desert iguana is brown and is smaller than the Green iguana. It lives in the deserts of Arizona, California, and Nevada.

19 Rhinoceros, or Rock, iguanas (left) are some of the biggest lizards around. They can be found on most Caribbean islands.

20 The Spiny-tailed iguana is also known as the Black iguana. It lives in Mexico and Central America, as well as on the islands near Panama.

21 The spines on an iguana's tail are scales that stand up, instead of lying flat like the scales on a fish or a snake. An iguana's spines help protect it from enemies.

22 Iguanas can use their tails to defend themselves. To scare off an enemy, an iguana will whip its tail from side to side. Sometimes it whips so hard that the tail breaks off!

23 An iguana's tail is built to break in certain places. When caught by an enemy, the iguana will break its tail off on purpose. The skin breaks with the bone to set the iguana free – and the tail grows back!

24 A pet iguana will behave much the same as an iguana in the wild. An iguana will never be a true house pet, like a cat or a dog, so think very carefully about it before you decide to buy one.

25 If you decide to buy an iguana, you will need to have a cage ready for it before you bring it home.

26 Pet iguanas can live in either a cage or a glass **terrarium** with a tight-fitting screen over the top. Cages are easier to move and clean, and they have better **ventilation**.

27 The cage for a 4-foot (1.2-m) iguana should be at least 6 feet (1.8 m) long, 6 feet (1.8 m) high, and 30 inches (76 cm) wide to give the iguana enough room.

28 You need to line the bottom of the cage with a suitable **substrate**, or covering material.

31 You should place your iguana's cage in a safe, quiet spot, away from other pets. Other animals frighten iguanas.

29 Newspapers, bark chips, gravel, and pieces of specially made carpeting are good substrates.

30 Do not use cat litter, household carpeting, wood shavings, or sand. They can get stuck in the iguana's stomach and cause blockage. They also hold bacteria, or germs, from the iguana's droppings. These germs can cause a chest infection.

33 When people stay in the sun too long, they usually get sunburned. Sunlight has **ultraviolet** (UV) rays that can burn things, but iguanas need these UV rays to stay healthy and active.

34 An iguana needs 6 to 12 hours of UV rays each day. If your iguana does not get enough natural sunlight, use a special reptile lamp or a fluorescent light. Both provide the UV rays iguanas need.

32 Also, be sure the cage is in a place where your iguana can get both natural sunlight and shade. Never put an iguana in the sun, however, when it is in a terrarium. The glass gets too hot, and the iguana will end up with heatstroke.

35 Natural light, of course, is always best, so take your iguana outside as much as possible in warm weather. Using a smaller, lightweight sunning cage can make it easier to carry your iguana outside.

36 Make sure that your iguana also gets out of the sun throughout the day. Iguanas can overheat or become **hyperactive** with too much natural sunlight.

37 You must control the temperature of your iguana's cage carefully. Use a thermometer to be sure.

38 The temperature of your iguana's cage should be between 85° and 90° Fahrenheit (29° and 32° Celsius) during the day. The temperature can be lower at night, but never let it fall below 65° F (18° C).

41 A good temperature for basking is 100° to 105° F (38° to 40° C).

42 Some iguana owners use hot rocks in a basking area, but they can get too hot and burn your pet.

43 Your iguana should also have an area in its cage where it can cool off.

39 If necessary, use a heat lamp or put a heating pad underneath your iguana's cage for warmth. Be sure you place the lamp outside the cage to keep the iguana from getting burned.

40 Iguanas like a place where they can **bask**, or sunbathe. A heat lamp focused on a thick tree branch makes a nice basking area.

14

iguana's cage so your pet can do some climbing.

46 After you have prepared a cage, you can buy your iguana. A large pet store or a breeder can offer you a wide choice.

44 Iguanas like to hide when they sleep and when they are afraid. Adding lots of plants to the cool spot in your pet's cage will make a great hiding place.

47 If you go to a pet store, make sure the store's employees know a lot about taking care of iguanas.

45 In the wild, many iguanas live in trees, so climbing comes naturally to them. Put a sturdy tree branch or a shelf inside your

15

48 Iguanas are very **territorial**, so you should buy only one. An iguana will fight if another iguana comes too close to its territory.

49 Some people would rather own female iguanas than males. Females do not seem to fight as much as males.

50 Male iguanas are bigger than females. A male usually has a wider head than a female, and the male's femoral pores are much larger.

51 The femoral pores are a single row of small round holes on the inside of an iguana's back legs. On a male iguana, the pores produce a waxy **discharge** that the male uses to mark its territory.

bones will be sticking out. A healthy iguana has a thick tail base and a solid, bright green body, and it flicks its tongue often. Do not buy an iguana that looks sleepy.

52 When you buy a pet iguana, a baby that is three to five months old is the best choice. At this age, iguanas are old enough to be strong and healthy but still young enough to handle changes well.

53 Make sure you buy a healthy iguana. If an iguana is sick, the place where its tail attaches to its body will be thin, and the

54 Do not buy an iguana that is not hungry, either. A healthy iguana has a good appetite.

55 Some other signs of an unhealthy iguana are a runny nose and swelling along the jaw.

56 Try not to buy an older iguana. It might have been returned to the pet store because of bad behavior. Ask the pet store manager why the iguana is being sold.

57 Never buy a wild iguana that has been captured to sell. Iguanas that are not tame may never get used to humans.

58 An iguana with a good personality will keep its eyes open, flick its tongue at you, and move around and stretch out a lot.

59 When you have chosen an iguana, take it home in a secure traveling container, such as a sturdy cardboard box that has a strong top with holes punched into it.

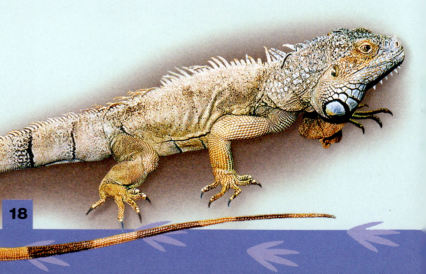

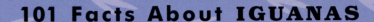

62 The correct way to hold an iguana is to firmly, but gently, support its chest and tail. Never grab it!

60 When you get your iguana home and into its cage, leave it alone for a week. The iguana needs this time to get used to its new home.

61 Although iguanas are naturally shy, they can be very affectionate after you earn their trust. Handle your pet iguana for at least a half hour each day so you can get to know each other.

63 Sometimes iguanas become so tame that they will sit on their owners' shoulders – like a parrot! Some iguanas will even wear a special leash, like a dog, and go for walks with their owners.

64 If your iguana is very tame, it will climb onto your hand. Most iguanas will become more tame if you hand-feed them.

65 In the wild, common iguanas are plant-eaters, or herbivores. Adults usually eat only plants, but babies eat mostly insects.

66 All of the food for your iguana needs to be soft or shredded. Food for a baby iguana should be mashed or **puréed**.

67 Iguanas need a lot of **calcium** in their diets. Calcium helps their bones grow properly.

68 To be sure that your pet iguana gets all the vitamins and minerals it needs, you should give it calcium carbonate and a multi-vitamin product. Pet stores have special tablets and liquids you can buy.

69 Just like people, iguanas like to eat a variety of foods. They can get bored with their diets if the food is always the same.

70 Your iguana might try to eat only what it likes. You have to make sure it also eats healthy foods.

71 Iguanas love lettuce, but it is "junk food" for them. Give your iguana lettuce only as a special treat.

72 Premixed food products that are sold for iguanas are not the best food for your pet. No more than one fifth of your iguana's total diet each week should be premixed food.

73 Feed your iguana mostly dark green, leafy vegetables, such as mustard or turnip greens. Other vegetables and many fruits are also healthy foods.

74 Baby iguanas really like human baby food – and it is good for them, too!

95 Some very serious problems that would need treatment by a reptile veterinarian include broken legs, bone and kidney diseases, and breathing problems.

96 Someday, your iguana might take care of you! A man in New York claims that his iguana saved his life. When the man had a heart attack, his iguana knocked the phone off the hook and accidently called for an ambulance.

97 Some people who have had iguanas for years like to breed them. Breeding is not hard, but it is better to leave it to the experts. For one thing, it requires a lot of room!

98 To breed iguanas, you need lots of cages for the babies. You also have to be sure that the male and female parents have plenty of space to stay out of each other's way. If they get too close to each other, they will fight.

93 All iguanas sneeze a lot, but if your iguana is sneezing more than normal, or if it is panting slightly, it might have a chest infection, and you should take it to a veterinarian.

91 Check the health of your iguana every day. Look to see if it has eaten all of its food and that it is alert.

94 Common problems you might have with your iguana are burns, cuts, mites, nose rubbing, and broken nails. A veterinarian can treat them all.

92 A runny nose, any lumps or swelling, color changes, and scratches or cuts on its skin are all signs of poor health.

Glossary

bask: lie in a warm place to relax.

calcium: a soft, grayish white, metallic mineral.

dehydrated: dried out from not having enough water.

digits: individual fingers and toes.

discharge: a thick or watery fluid that seeps through an opening.

ectothermic: cold-blooded; receiving body heat from an outside source.

endangered: in danger of dying out completely as a species.

habitats: the places where animals normally live in nature.

hyperactive: overly active.

lukewarm: just barely warm.

puréed: mashed or whipped into a thin, almost liquid, paste.

salmonella: a kind of bacteria, or germ, that causes serious stomach problems and fevers that make people very sick.

species: a particular group, or type, of animals that are alike in many ways.

substrate: a covering material that forms a foundation, or base, on which an animal can live.

terrarium: a glass-sided container that looks like an aquarium but is not filled with water.

territorial: on guard to protect an area claimed as private property.

ultraviolet: an invisible ray of sunlight at the violet end of the light spectrum.

ventilation: air movement that replaces stale air with fresh air.

100 Both male and female iguanas have crests. Only a male iguana, however, can raise, or ruffle, its scales to make its crest look bigger.

101 Iguanas may be unusual pets, but if they are given good care, they can be just as friendly and fun as cats and dogs.

99 When a male and a female iguana are mating – or fighting – the male will show off its crest, which is a row of large, pointed scales that run down the length of its back.

Index

babies 5, 17, 20, 21, 22, 28
bathing 14, 23, 24
breeding 28

cages 10, 11, 12, 13, 14, 15,
   19, 23, 25, 28
claws, nails 6, 26, 27
cleaning 10, 23, 25
climbing 15, 20, 24
colors 7, 27
crests 29

eyes 7, 18

females 5, 16, 28, 29
fighting 16, 28, 29
food 20, 21, 22, 27

health 12, 17, 18, 22, 23,
   25, 27
heat 4, 12, 13, 14

lizards 4, 5, 8

males 16, 28, 29

reptiles 4, 12, 24, 26, 28

salmonella 24
scales 9, 29
shedding 25
sleeping 15, 17
sneezing 27
species 4, 5
sunlight 12, 13
swimming 24

tails 6, 9, 17, 19

veterinarians 26, 27, 28
vitamins, minerals 21

water 23, 24, 25

More Books to Read

Becoming Best Friends with Your Iguana, Snake, or Turtle
Bill Gutman (Millbrook Press)

Iguanas (Exotic Lizards series)
W. P. Mara
(Capstone Press)

My Pet Iguana
Amy Adams
(Shining Lights Press)

Your Pet Iguana
Elaine Landau
(Children's Press)

Web Sites

Green Iguana Society: Kids Club
www.greenigsociety.org/
kidsclub.htm

Green Iguanas: The Basics
www.peteducation.com/ig_liz/
iguanas_basics.htm

Iguana Iguana: A Newsletter for Lizard Lovers
www.iguana-news.com

Little Lucy's Page
members.aol.com/mylittlelu

To find additional web sites, use a reliable search engine, such as www.yahooligans.com, with one or more of the following keywords: **green iguana, iguana, iguana care, lizards, reptiles**.